GROWING PEONIES FROM SEED

Grow your Blossom Peony flowers, Outdoor and Indoor Peony Seeds Germination.

MICHAEL GRONNY

Copyright 2021 Morgan.

This book is subject to copyright policy. All rights are reserved, whether the entire or component of the material, particularly the right of transformation, reprinting, recycling illustration, broadcasting, duplicating on microfilm, or in any other way. No part or even the whole of this book or contents may be produced or even transmitted or reproduced in any way, be it electronic or paper form or by any means, electronic or mechanical, also include recording or by any information storage or retrieval system, without prior written permission the copyright owner, *Morgan LTD*

TABLE OF CONTENTS

GROW PEONIES FROM SEEDS 2
INTRODUCTION 7
PART 1: UNDERSTANDING PEONY FLOWERS 9
WHERE DO PEONIES COME FROM? 10
PEONIES FLOWER IN UK 11
WHAT MAKES PEONIES SPECIAL FROM OTHER FLOWERS 12
PART 2: CATEGORIES AND TYPES: PEONY PLANTS, BLOOMS COLORS 15
CATEGORY OF PEONY PLANTS 15
CATEGORY OF PEONY FLOWER BLOOMS 16
PEONY FLOWER COLORS 17
HERBACEOUS PEONIES 18
VARIETY OF HERBACEOUS PEONIES 19
TREE PEONIES 20
INTERSECTIONAL PEONIES 21

PART 3: EXPERT TIPS AND TRICKS TO GROW YOUR PEONIES 23
BEST TIME TO PLANT YOUR PEONIES: 23
DEEP AND SHALLOW PLANTING TIPS: 23
WHERE DO PEONIES GROW BEST? 24
HOW LONG DOES IT PEONIES TO FOWER AND HOW LONG DOES IT LIVE? 25
HOW TO MOVE AND REPLANT YOUR PEONIES. ...26

PART 4: CUTTING PEONIES AND FLOWER ARRANGEMENT 28
GETTING RID OF ANTS ON PEONIES 29

PART 5: REASONS YOUR PEONIES ARE NOT FLOWERING 31

PART 6: GERMINATE AND GROW PEONIES OUTDOOR 33
WHAT YOU NEED TO KNOW: 35
STEP 1: PEONY SEED PREPARATION: 36
STEP 2: PEONY SEEDS (FRESH SEEDS VS DRY SEEDS): 37
STEP 3: CHOOSE A PLANTING SITE WITH AT LEAST ½ DAY SUNLIGHT: 38
STEP 4: SOIL MOISTURE: 39
STEP 6: COVER THE BED WITH WOOD CHIPS: 41
STEP 7: USE A SHEET OF CLEAR PLASTIC: 42
STEP 8: YOU NEED TO BE PATIENT: 43

PART 7: GROW PEONIES FROM SEEDS INDOOR PROCEDURE 45
SOIL AND PLANTING THE SEEDS: 45
STORAGE AND SUITABLE LOCATION: 45
NURSERY BED IN THE GARDEN: 46
YOUR FIRST LEAVES: 47
PEONY FLOWERS: 47

INTRODUCTION

Are you having difficulties in starting peonies from seed or are you having difficulties on how you can start your first Peony plants? Peonies are easy to germinate from seed, but it takes a longer period of time between 1-3 years or even more than. The result is considered very rewarding if properly done. There are some ways that we have discovered to be effective for growing peonies.

In this book, we will discuss various steps on how you can grow peonies from seed and also everything you will need to know about peonies including the tips, tricks, and approaches to achieve blossom peonies.

A healthy tree peony may produce more than 50 seeds per pod. Only few plants can compete with the robust and blossom peonies, whose massive flowers may be as large as dinner plates.

PART 1: UNDERSTANDING PEONY FLOWERS

The peony flowers are beautiful flower plant that belongs to the genus *Paeonia*, which is the sole genus in the *Paeoniaceae group*. Asia, Europe, as well as Western North America are all homes to peonies.

WHERE DO PEONIES COME FROM?

Peonies (Paeonia) are flowering plants that can be found in Asia, Europe, as well as North America. The peony is the floral emblem of China as well as the state flower of Indiana, thus it has a lot of cultural value.

Peony flower comes in 33 distinct varieties and they are considered to signify good fortune as well as a happy marriage. They are a popular choice for bridal bouquets as well as the official flower for the twelfth-anniversary celebration.

PEONIES FLOWER IN UK

One thing you will need to know about peony is that it has a very short flowering season. Therefore, making it very expensive and also in high demand once it becomes blossom.

In the united kingdom, between a period of late April and early June peony flowers are at their best in the month of May.

WHAT MAKES PEONIES SPECIAL FROM OTHER FLOWERS

The followings are reasons why we see peonies as special flowers compare to others:

Peonies are signs of Wealth Honor.	In history till date peonies have been traditionally known as a sign of honor, romance, wealth, and love. They are also known as a symbol of marriage.
12th anniversary Flower.	They are popularly known for their 12th-anniversary flower.
Long period.	Peony's flower lives for long. Peonies can live for more than 1000 years and still look blossom.
Toronto peonies.	Peonies bloom from late May through June in Toronto.
Native flower	Peonies are known to be native flowers in Asia, Western North America as well as Southern Europe.
Naming	The word Peony is named after Paeon also spelled Paean
sho yu	In Chinese peonies are known to be *sho yu* which

	simply means "most beautiful".
White Peony	The white peony is known to be the oldest remedy in traditional Chinese medicine.

PART 2: CATEGORIES AND TYPES: PEONY PLANTS, BLOOM COLORS

CATEGORY OF PEONY PLANTS

Peony plants fall into three main categories. Which are:

- Herbaceous peonies.
- Tree peonies.
- Intersectional/ Itoh peonies.

The shape of the peony flower differs. Some range mostly from airy, frilly pom-pom puffs as well as some is made up of delicate to bodacious blooms.

CATEGORY OF PEONY FLOWER BLOOMS

Bloom peony flowers are made up of six (6) types:

- Single

- Japanese
- Anemone
- Semi-Double
- Bombe
- Ful double

PEONY FLOWER COLORS

Peonies have different colors it all depends on what you want and the colors depend on the species. Several peonies have Pinks mix with white flowers while some are White, Purple, red and sometimes we see orange and yellow peony flowers. These vary from different types.

HERBACEOUS PEONIES

The most common kind of peony is the herbaceous peony. Each spring has diminutive plants that produce a blossom of flowers before withering back to the ground. During early spring, new stems begin to grow in preparation for the next late bloom period.

VARIETY OF HERBACEOUS PEONIES

There are a lot of varieties of herbaceous peonies. We have:

Sarah Bernhardt penny	Bowl of beauty penny	Goldilocks peony
Festival Maxima peony	Coral charm peony	Shirley temple
Dinner plate	Paula fay	Red charm

| peony | peony | peony |
| Belgravia peony | Raspberry peony | Fernleaf peony |

TREE PEONIES

Peonies that grow on a persistent woody stalk are known as tree peonies. The tree peony is quite like a resistant shrub than the more typical herbaceous peonies, which have stems that die down to the ground every autumn. Woody stems survive the winter and return to blossom the following season. The followings are a variety of tree peonies:

High noon tree peony	Shima Nishiki tree peony
Renkaku tree peony	Shima daijin tree peony

INTERSECTIONAL PEONIES

The intersectional peonies are also known as the *Itoh peonies* with features of large, beautiful foliage as well as fragrant flowers. This type of peony is tolerant to high temperatures during cool or warm weather and maintaining a compact growth habit. There are bred as crosses mostly between woody type tree and herbaceous peonies.

The follows are a variety of intersectional peonies:

First arrival Itoh peony	Hillary Itoh peony	Julia rose itoh peony
Lollipop Itoh peony	Cora Louise Itoh peony	Garden treasure peony

PART 3: EXPERT TIPS AND TRICKS TO GROW YOUR PEONIES

Below are tips and tricks to grow your peonies:

BEST TIME TO PLANT YOUR PEONIES:

The actual time that is more suitable during the year to plant your peonies is between October and March. However, some experts are against planting peonies during December.

DEEP AND SHALLOW PLANTING TIPS:

The most essential factor is how deep you will plant your peonies; if you put them too deep, they will not blossom. Herbaceous peonies should be planted with blooming stems not more than 2cm below the soil surface.

WHERE DO PEONIES GROW BEST?

Despite the popular belief that surrounds growing peony flowers. Peony plants are easy to grow as far as the basic things are done. Peonies need watering, so plant your peonies in soil that drains well. Clay soil is suitable for peonies as far as it does not stay wet all the time.

You need to also put the level of temperature into considerations like sunshine and light shade.

HOW LONG DOES IT TAKE PEONIES TO FLOWER AND HOW LONG DOES IT LIVE?

It depends but some take up to 3years to start striding and flowering freely. Peonies live for up to 30-50years depending on the type and they are easy to adapt to a new environment.

HOW TO TRANSPLANT YOUR PEONIES.

- It is easy to move and replant your peonies.
- Ensure that the peony plant is dormant that is the best time to move when it is dormant.
- This should be done between October and March.
- Start by digging around the roots. Please, make sure that the roots are not mistakenly cut.

- Thereafter uproot as little of the rootball as possible.
- Next is to transplant them to their new environment.

PART 4: CUTTING PEONIES AND FLOWER ARRANGEMENT

Peonies produce lovely cut flowers as well as may stay up to 10 days in a vase even longer than garden roses.

Patience is required if you wish to develop peonies from cutting. The majority of cut cultivars might take up to three years to develop enough flowers for cutting. However, because the blooms are so enormous, the ordinary vase only requires one or two flowers to appear lovely and incredibly opulent.

GETTING RID OF ANTS ON PEONIES

What to do to get rid of ants on peony flower bud is a common question. Some experts have said that it does not harm or destroy the flower. Ants, in my experience! Do not harm. They appear when the bud grows and feed on the sweet fluid it emits, maybe even assisting the bud in fully opening. The ant goes as soon as the buds begin to emerge.

PART 5: REASONS YOUR PEONIES ARE NOT FLOWERING

Planting a peony too deeply is the most common reason why your peonies are not flowering. Herbaceous peonies should be planted with the eyes (blooming stems) not more than 2cm below the soil surface. Peony leaves will thrive even if planted too deeply, but they will not yield flowers.

If this happened to be the reason then you will have to wait until autumn before you attempt to start uprooting the plant and replanting it in a portable position.

PART 6: GERMINATE AND GROW PEONIES OUTDOOR

I remembered when I first started, one of the most unforgettable moments that I have ever had during my flower garden was seeing my first peony seedling growing and turning out flowers. It takes a lot of time for your peonies flower to start growing that is why when I first saw it I was very happy.

In this chapter, I will show you how you can plant your first peonies from seed and also everything you need to know about the germination of peony seeds.

One of the best way to plant as well as grow peony seeds is by planting the seed outdoors. When they are ripe or during late summer when we have dry seeds some of the seeds do emerge to be spring while some will require an additional year.

WHAT YOU NEED TO KNOW:

The followings are things you need to put into consideration before you start the process of growing your peony flowers.

- Firstly, growing a blossom peony flower takes a lot of time 3-5 years to flower.
- The process requires caring, weeding, and watering.
- Peony seeds are gotten from the pods when the flower dies off the plant.
- When the seed ripens the pods crack off.
- You will need a moderate temperature as well as moisture.

The followings are steps you will need to follow to achieve blossom peonies:

STEP 1: PEONY SEED PREPARATION:

The first thing you need to do is to get your seed pods and ensure that they are ripened or better still you can leave them on the plants for them to be ripe. Wait until they are harden as well as start to open to show the seeds. Now is the moment for you to gather them.

To start the process of germinating, the seeds will require a period for moist warmth for a few weeks or even months, they will need a period of winter for around 10 to 12 weeks.

STEP 2: PEONY SEEDS (FRESH SEEDS VS DRY SEEDS):

Fresh seeds are planted as soon as possible after harvest. Dry seeds gotten during the winter and spring should be planted in the middle of the summer. Because dry seed requires a longer period to be hydrated than fresh seed as well as hard or strong seeds are difficult to crack, they are kept in wet warm soil for extended period of time.

STEP 3: CHOOSE A PLANTING SITE WITH AT LEAST ½ DAY SUNLIGHT:

Choose your peony planting location or site that gets at least ½ of sunshine each day throughout the growing season and well-drained. In addition, the site should be shielded from drying winds and extreme heat or sunshine.

The site will be used as a nursery bed, providing ideal growing conditions for young plants throughout their 1-5 years of existence

STEP 4: SOIL MOISTURE:

Start by cultivating the site you want to plant your peony seeds to fine texture. Ensure that the soil are moist and make sure it is not too wet.

STEP 5: PLANTING PROCESS:

In this stage be ready to plant your peonies;

- Start by pressing the peony seeds into the outer surface of the soil.
- The depth should not be more than ½ inch.
- You don't need to cover the peony seeds with the soil rather make it firm and pack in the surface of the soil.
- For a better outcome, you will need to space seeds one to two inches;

this will enable it to conserve space in the controlled bed.
- Spacing is essential because you will require taking care of your peonies (weeding and watering).
- You will require a long-lasting garden marker in the seedbed. This will enable you to identify plants during the growing process.
- It is also essential for you to continuously know the identity of what comes up in the bed. You may need it in the future and it could be shared or distributed later on.

STEP 6: COVER THE BED WITH WOOD CHIPS:

Cover the bed with fine wood chips, wood/bark/mulch, sawdust, or wood shavings, about one inch thick. The wood mulch will preserve the bed moist as well as provide some protection from the elements for the early plant stage. Young peonies seem to have a strong attraction to rotting wood, which encourages growth.

STEP 6: USE A SHEET OF CLEAR PLASTIC:

Use a sheet of clear plastic to cover the bed and it is also essential that you bury the edges of the plastic with soil to enable seal. The sealing should be done in such a way that it wouldn't be easy to pull out by wind or other factors. The bed covering should be left throughout the winter as well as removed as soon as necessary during the spring.

STEP 8: YOU NEED TO BE PATIENT:

Young seedlings will sprout. Seedlings can take up to three years to develop or emerge in the bed, so be patient. The plants will only generate a single leaf in the first season. Keep them properly hydrated (but not too wet) and out of direct sunlight. The seedlings will have grown considerably enough to transplant in early fall with increased space in them if the bed is maintained undisturbed for two to three years. Some may blossom in the third year, some in the fourth, as well as the stragglers in the fifth and sixth. The majority of them will bloom in year four if they are adequately cared for.

PART 7: GROW PEONIES FROM SEED INDOOR PROCEDURE

The followings are the procedures to follow when growing your indoor peonies seeds:

SOIL AND PLANTING THE SEEDS:

Firstly, during the starting of October. Get a food storage bag and fill up to 2-4 moist soil. Ensure that the planting of the seeds should be 4cm apart as well as 2-21/2cm deep inside the bag.

STORAGE AND SUITABLE LOCATION:

Place the food-storage plastic bags in a suitable place with moderate temperature and water it. Location in a warm place (about 20 degrees Celsius) for around 3 months as well as a knot with a twist tie. The radicle, as well as a root system, will grow at this time. Without hurting the little plants, the soil may be carefully removed for occasional inspection. Simply refill the dirt and reseal the bags.

Place the bag in a cool location after the radicles, as well as roots, have grown sufficiently. Keep it in a cold temperature for two, three, or four months until SPRING!

NURSERY BED IN THE GARDEN:

In this aspect consider choosing a site in the garden for your main nursery bed.

Carefully knock the soil as well as seedlings out of the bag. Ensure that the depth of the plant should be too deep. Next is for you to insert a plant marker with detail of seedling information. Ensure that your planting is done in an area with moist (mulch).

YOUR FIRST LEAVES:

The first leaves will develop over the summer. Some seedlings may not sprout leaves until the next spring. Wait patiently.

Leave the little plants throughout the winter (more layers of mulch will allow them to survive the winter without heaving) through August to September the subsequent year.

At this point, transplant 1 foot apart as well as at the same depth as the plant is growing.

PEONY FLOWERS:

If properly done you may have blossom flowers 3rd year. In year 4 or 5, you should expect a lot of flowers. What a joy! What a sense of accomplishment to see your first peony blossom from your own plants.

Printed in Great Britain
by Amazon